KICKSTARTER AND PATREON

JUSTINE CIOVACCO

rosen publishing's
rosen central®

New York

Published in 2017 by The Rosen Publishing Group, Inc.
29 East 21st Street, New York, NY 10010

Library of Congress Cataloging-in-Publication Data

Names: Ciovacco, Justine, author.
Title: Kickstarter and Patreon / Justine Ciovacco.
Description: First edition. | New York : Rosen Publishing, 2017. | Series:
Digital and information literacy | Includes bibliographical references and index.
Identifiers: LCCN 2016017425| ISBN 9781508173311 (library bound) | ISBN
9781508173519 (pbk.) | ISBN 9781508173304 (6-pack)
Subjects: LCSH: Crowd funding—Juvenile literature. | Venture
capital—Juvenile literature. | New business
enterprises—Finance—Juvenile literature. | Social media—Juvenile literature.
Classification: LCC HG4751 .C56 2017 | DDC 658.15/224—dc23
LC record available at https://lccn.loc.gov/2016017425

Manufactured in China

CONTENTS

INTRODUCTION

Have you ever dreamed of starting your own business? Or maybe you have thought about how something you created could be really popular? If only people knew about it, that is. Are you an artist with a unique vision? You might need money to complete a project. Perhaps you want to help someone low on cash. You might want to encourage other people to pitch in, too. Everyone has great ideas. But we don't all have the time, energy, and money to make them a reality. Crowdfunding allows people to do all of these things.

Crowdfunding is a popular way to raise small amounts of money. It comes from a large number of people, usually via the internet. People have been giving to others for centuries. But crowdfunding is big business now. The term *crowdfunding* even made it into the Oxford English Dictionary in 2015. So did the words *photobombing* and *twerking*. Dance moves like twerking can easily lose their cool factor. Crowdfunding seems to be here to stay, though.

More than 1,250 websites have been developed to raise money for new businesses and others in need. New campaigns pop up on these sites every day. Some fail. Others succeed and become viral sensations. News articles around the world cover these all the time.

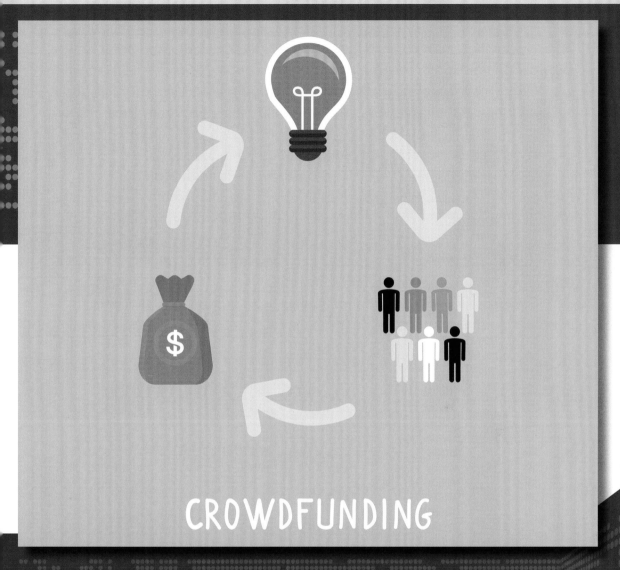

CROWDFUNDING

Crowdfunding is a concept in which ideas are presented to the public, who then provides funding so the ideas can become reality.

Crowdfunding is an amazing resource. It helps people and small businesses that don't normally get much press. Many worthy causes and efforts have a hard time getting the news out about themselves.

Crowdfunding can help. It provides aspiring entrepreneurs with amazing help. By getting them funding, these business people can accomplish a lot. They can perfect a marketing pitch. Or get valuable feedback from possible customers. They can also gain positive attention for their work. Artists attract a global audience for the work. This can help them reach new fans. It can also nudge existing fans to invest in new efforts.

People often want to help others with personal needs. Every day, people lose their homes. Their loved ones die and need to be buried. Animals get sick. Charities need money to carry on their work. The list goes on and on. Crowdfunding can act as a microphone. It sends out messages and gathers like-minded supporters. Some of the most popular crowdfunding platforms are websites like Kickstarter and Patreon. They act as bridges between people's modern wants, needs, and pipe dreams.

Social media and crowdfunding sites have made it easier to reach people around the world. Yet their real strength is in linking people with common interests. Everyone has ideas. It's a lot easier to make them reality with the support of other people's time, energy, and money.

Chapter 1

How Does Crowdfunding Work?

People have given money to artists, entrepreneurs, and those in need since time began. Tithing is one means of this. An individual gives money (perhaps a portion of income) to religious organizations and houses of worship. This form of giving is discussed in the Bible and other ancient texts. Centuries ago, explorers such as Christopher Columbus and Marco Polo needed money for their journeys. Rich and royal patrons stepped up to the plate. Likewise, artists like Leonardo da Vinci had wealthy patrons. They often provided money for exciting new projects.

Leonardo da Vinci was one of many artists who was given financial support by wealthy patrons who backed his creative projects.

Crowdfunding is different. The key to its success is that not just the rich and powerful give to a cause. It gathers attention and, often, small amounts of money from a large number of sources. Today, it is a style of fundraising that uses websites and social media to gather support. Support comes from many sources. Examples are friends, fans, and people who take an interest in certain causes.

Each project is usually called a campaign. It begins with the ideas of a person or number of people. They have needs and the desire to reach others. The campaigners, or content creators, list information about their project. They include a bit about themselves and the history of their project. They also give a plan for how they will use the money.

Most sites offer rewards for people who give their money to a particular effort. This can be as simple as listing their names (if they chose), funding amounts, and comments. Other rewards, such as limited-edition products, can also be given to contributors.

The Early History of Crowdfunding

Forget for a moment the way crowdfunding is conducted today. The internet wasn't always around. Using small amounts of money to fund big projects has happened before crowdfunding existed. One of these examples involves the building of the Statue of Liberty. The mighty copper lady in New York Harbor wouldn't exist without this effort. It involved the financial support of many people and a well-planned campaign to attract those donations.

French sculptor Frédéric Auguste Bartholdi had a vision. He wanted to design a giant lighthouse in the shape of a woman. In the late 1860s, he tried to get an Egyptian leader to fund the building of a statue of a robed peasant woman holding a lamp at an entrance to the Suez Canal. He failed. By 1871, though, he turned his attention to the idea of a similar monument in another place. This one would stand in New York City. It would be given to the people of the United States by the French as a symbol of freedom. Bartholdi felt it should be funded as a joint French-American project. The French government agreed to pay for the statue to be built by popular French architect Gustave Eiffel of Eiffel Tower fame. It was up to the Americans to fund the $250,000 granite base for the statue.

A group called the American Committee of the Statue of Liberty collected nearly $150,000. They needed more, though. New York governor Grover Cleveland, who later became a president of the United States, played a role in it. He wouldn't approve the use of city funds for the statue's base. The US Congress could not put together enough votes for funding. At last, a man with a plan saved the day. Publisher Joseph Pulitzer declared he would launch a fundraising campaign. He would do it in his popular newspaper, *The New York World*. In five months, more than 160,000 donors raised the remaining money. Three-quarters of the funding came from donations that were less than a dollar.

Like today's crowdfunding efforts, the funding of the Statue of Liberty used a single collection point. In this case, it was the newspaper, which attracted interest and small amounts of money from a wide range of people. It also

Joseph Pulitzer started an early crowdfunding campaign by using his newspaper to promote public funding for the construction of the Statue of Liberty.

used the media—here, it was print—to keep a tally of contributions. The newspaper listed the amounts given by everyone, whether big or small. One example inspired a lot of attention. The newspaper listed the story of Philip Bender, a father in Jersey City, New Jersey, on March 22, 1885. He broke down his family's $2.65 donation. He and his wife gave 50 cents each. The remaining $1.65 came from the donations of their eight children and other family members. The newspaper also offered rewards, including gold coins for the largest donor. Most importantly, like today's crowdfunding campaigns, the money for this early success was also raised quickly!

Funding Goes Digital

It's hard to pinpoint the exact start of modern crowdfunding. Charities have been collecting donations online since it became possible to do so. Crowdfunding sites not connected to charities also exist. Artists and musicians set up efforts to promote their own work early on in the history of the internet. Such sites have grown and multiplied as word got out of their success.

One of the earliest crowdfunding projects broke new ground in 1997. Fans of the British rock band Marillion raised $60,000. This came from an internet-based effort started by fans. They hoped to fund a North American tour after the band's record label went bankrupt. The talk of funding the tour began with fans writing on fan sites and the band's website. Mass emails from fans also helped alert other fans to the need for funding.

The original goal was $30,000. But Marillion fans from around the world raised $47,000 between February and September 1997. Marillion responded by putting together a twenty-one-date North American tour. "The band became aware for the first time that there were fans who would put the money where their hearts are," singer Steve Hogarth told BBC News in 2001. "It came as a bit of a shock to all five of us—even though we knew about the strength of feeling from the atmosphere at the shows."

The success amazed and inspired the band. They had just fulfilled a three-album deal on an independent record label in 2001. The new deals they were being offered didn't impress them, though. They decided to take their plans for a new album to the internet. "I wrote an email with words to the effect of 'how would you guys feel about buying a record we haven't made yet—because if you did, we'd be really grateful'," said Hogarth.

His simple sales pitch was enough. In just two days, six thousand fans responded. About twelve thousand fans preordered the band's next album. Called *Anoraknophobia*, their twelfth album sold for £15 each (about $21). The band then made a deal with the international record label EMI. EMI would market and distribute the album.

"The fact the fans financed this record gave us a warm feeling inside when we were making it," said Hogarth. "And it gave us a feeling of

The progressive rock band Marillion, whose 1997 crowdfunding campaign inspired today's internet-based crowdfunding platforms, is seen here in 2015.

responsibility to make something special… Without them we would cease to exist overnight."

Anoraknophobia was the first crowdfunded album. But it was far from the last. A Boston musician named Brian Camelio came up with a similar effort in the United States. The internet startup site called ArtistShare opened in 2003. On it, musicians could attract donations from fans to produce digital recordings. Today, the site raises funds for film and photography projects as well.

File   Edit   View   Favorites   Tools   Help

WHAT IS AN INTERNET STARTUP?

What Is an Internet Startup?

Crowdfunding sites develop in a way similar to the projects they promote. They take a lot of time, energy, and money to be created and become successful.

A startup company—internet or otherwise—is a new business. It takes the form of a company that develops a new business model. This new model comes about because of a problem that exists that needs a solution. Startups try to find solutions by creating a company to work on them. Whether this will fail is always a risk.

Internet startups take shape every day all over the world. They are not meant to be stable business models. Instead, they are based on the idea that hard work, fresh ideas, and money can fix problems and create new services. There are some huge crowdfunding sites today. Each of them was a startup at one time.

Sites can still be considered startups as late as three years into development. The success of a startup usually comes when the site is bought by a larger company. Often it will have more than one office or more than eighty employees. Startups that bring in profits greater than $20 million are also successes.

ArtistShare's first crowdfunding project was a jazz album. It was created by composer Maria Schneider and called *Concert in a Garden*. She offered a tiered system of rewards. For $9.95, a backer could be among the first to download the album upon its release. Fans who gave $250 or more would get the download. They would also have the honor of being listed in the booklet as people who "helped to make this recording possible." A $10,000 contribution meant that a fan was listed as executive producer.

Schneider's campaign raised almost $130,000. This allowed her to take time off from other work. She could then compose the music, pay her musicians, and rent a recording studio. Producing and marketing the album was also a priority. In 2005, it won a Grammy Award for best large jazz ensemble album.

The success of ArtistShare helped other crowdfunding platforms to grow. The most popular among these include Indiegogo in 2008, Kickstarter in 2009, GoFundMe in 2010, and Patreon in 2013.

Chapter 2

A Closer Look at Kickstarter

Kickstarter is one of the first and most popular crowdfunding sites. It aims to help creators find the funding and support they need to turn their ideas into reality. Creators can be artists, musicians, filmmakers, designers, or others.

From its launch in 2009 through April 2016, Kickstarter boasts a huge number of funding campaigns. It has hosted more than 265,000, in fact. Of those, 102,606 succeeded. They raised a total of $2.3 billion from more than 10.6 million backers. Most successful campaigns raise less than $10,000. Yet about 29 percent of them raised more than $10,000. About 2.6 percent raised more than $100,000.

The site claims that more than eleven million people have backed a Kickstarter project. They have come from every continent on Earth. Who are these backers? As is true on many such sites, lots of them are friends and family of the campaigners. Those people are important because they help spread the word about the projects. Some people want to see creative people's dreams come true. And some just want a piece of the finished product. Still, backers are a dedicated group. There are 10.6 million

Kickstarter (www.kickstarter.com) is one of the best-known crowdfunding sites, having launched in 2009.

backers registered on Kickstarter from its start to April 2016. More than 3 million of these are repeat backers. This means they have supported multiple projects.

One thing that is interesting about who is backing Kickstarter projects is the age range of visitors. Most—35 percent—are thirty-five to forty-four years old. Those who are twenty-five to thirty-four years old are close behind at 27 percent. People in these age ranges tend to be active internet users, but they earn their own money, unlike many younger site visitors. Only about 12 percent of the site's visitors are fifty-five and older.

Anyone can bring ideas to the site. Many famous people have, including actor and producer Whoopi Goldberg, performance artist Marina Abramović, and director Spike Lee. Yet many creators are artists, bands, and filmmakers you've never heard of. Each creator develops his or her own project, as well as the funding goal and deadline.

Who Runs It

Kickstarter is currently managed by a team of 136 people. They are based in Greenpoint, Brooklyn, a borough of New York City. About half of these people design and code the site. The other half work with the campaigners and backers. The creative office is dog friendly with a few pups making the daily commute with their humans.

Kickstarter co-founders Yancey Strickler, Perry Chen, and Charles Adler needed to fund their start-up site with millions of dollars from investors.

The site launched on April 29, 2009. Its founders are entrepreneurs Perry Chen, Charles Adler, and Yancy Strickler. Chen is an artist himself. The site really took off with about $10 million in funding from investors. They saw its worth and potential growth as a site to help artists and small businesses. In 2010, *Time* magazine named the site one of the "best inventions of 2010."

Although Kickstarter started in the United States, it began to open to projects in the United Kingdom in 2012. This was quickly followed by projects in Canada, Australia, Italy, Ireland, Norway, France, Sweden, and Spain, among others.

How It Works

Kickstarter has an all-or-nothing model, favored by many crowdfunding sites. All-or-nothing means that if a project does not reach its stated funding goal within a certain time period, it fails. The funders' credit cards are not charged, so even Kickstarter itself earns nothing. Indiegogo is one site that allows both all-or-nothing and keep-it-all campaigns. In the latter, the project may keep all the funds it raises even if the goal is not reached.

It's important to note that the majority of Kickstarter campaigners come away with no funding. Only about 36 percent of projects are fully funded. This opens a world of opportunity for the most fortunate and talented campaigners.

The most successful projects on Kickstarter are by far music and film/video. The next most popular projects include art, publishing, games, design, and theater, among other categories. Kickstarter charges a fee of 5 percent of the funds collected in a fully funded campaign. Plus, Amazon Payments, which processes contributions, takes another 3 to 5 percent.

Kickstarter Success Stories

Success for Kickstarter is measured in popularity and pledges. After all, popular campaigns bring new backers to the site, and pledges keep it in business!

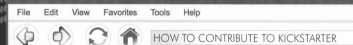

How to Contribute to Kickstarter

Kickstarter makes contributing to projects—and finding out about those that interest you—easy. They recommend a list of projects based on people's interests. Other projects are featured in the newsletter. The site makes social media connections easy. It also offers advanced search options.

To pledge, you create an account on the site. Next you search for projects. Each campaign's page has a big green Back This Project button. Clicking here brings you to a list of rewards and related funding tiers. You may need to pay for shipping of rewards, but you may also opt out of receiving any reward. This option generally saves the campaigners money.

You must use a debit or credit card to pay for pledges. The site doesn't accept PayPal.

The most successful Kickstarter campaign by far was for the Pebble smart watch (Pebble Time). A group of entrepreneurs from Palo Alto, California, developed a digital wristwatch. It features a microphone, runs sports and fitness apps, and wirelessly connects to a smartphone. The goal was $500,000 to be funded by March 2015. Backers could preorder the watch. This helped excited backers build up to the goal within the first seventeen minutes of the campaign. In the end, the campaign raised an incredible $20.4 million from 78,741 backers.

Another amazingly successful campaign was the Coolest Cooler in 2014. This was based on the plan for a multifunction cooler that crushes ice. It also has a USB charging port, Bluetooth water-resistant speaker, and LED lamps. The fundraising goal was $50,000. It banked a much more massive $13,285,000 from 62,000 backers. What was especially notable

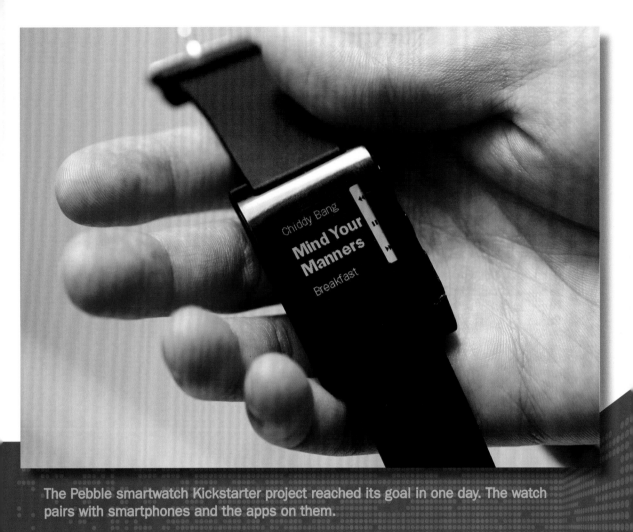

The Pebble smartwatch Kickstarter project reached its goal in one day. The watch pairs with smartphones and the apps on them.

was that many backers pledged amounts less than the minimum required to get a reward. They weren't expecting a tangible reward. Instead, they simply wanted to support the product and its campaigners.

Even Oscar-nominated directors can find success on Kickstarter. Filmmaker Spike Lee raised $1.4 million from 6,421 backers in August 2013. This was to make an unnamed film he told fans little about. The thriller, he said, was about people addicted to blood. In return for funding, backers were promised downloads of the film. They could also receive autographed memorabilia from past Spike Lee films.

Lee's name recognition brought a lot attention, but not all of it was good. Actor, writer, and director Zach Braff learned this, too. In May 2013, he started an ultimately successful campaign. It brought in $3.1 million to fund the film *Wish I Was Here*. Many people were irritated that the rich and

Director Spike Lee (left), promoting his first Kickstarter-funded film with its featured actress Zaraah Abrahams, offered backers memorabilia from his past films.

famous wanted to use the site. Yet the rich and famous have argued that they, too, can't always get the funding to do exactly what they envision.

Lee was inspired to use the site for the film that he later named *Da Sweet Blood of Jesus* (2014) after a student in his New York University film class suggested it. Lee had been complaining about how hard it was to get Hollywood to fund the unique films he wanted to make. "The truth is I've been doing KICKSTARTER before there was KICKSTARTER, there was no Internet," Lee wrote to backers in answer to complaints. "[Back then] social media was writing letters, making phone calls, beating the bushes. I'm now using TECHNOLOGY with what I've been doing."

In terms of awards, at least five Kickstarter-funded documentary shorts have been nominated for Oscars. One, Inocente, won in 2013. Many more films funded by the site have been accepted at major film festivals, such as Sundance and South by Southwest (SXSW).

Do It Yourself

You, too, may be able to start a Kickstarter campaign. But time, creativity, and the ability to see your project through are essential. The site accepts only 60 percent of the two thousand or so projects offered by hopefuls each week. Kickstarter also lists requirements that all creators must follow. Included in these are that you must be eighteen years old, a permanent resident of one of the site's approved countries, and have an address and bank account in the country in which you are creating the project.

Before launching a project, the site suggests people do the following:

- Make a detailed budget of costs. This is necessary to set a funding goal.
- Study other Kickstarter projects, particularly those recommended by the site.

- Brainstorm about what rewards you can realistically offer.
- Read the Creator Handbook.
- Have a plan to spread the word about the project.

One tricky thing to consider is how much you can tell people about your project. You must be open to encourage people to support you. Giving away too much information can hinder the uniqueness of the project. "Being open and sharing ideas is an essential part of Kickstarter," the site explains. "If you don't want to share much information with potential backers then Kickstarter probably isn't for you."

TEN GREAT QUESTIONS

TO ASK A CAMPAIGN ORGANIZER

Here are some great questions to ask a campaigner who lists projects on these sites.

1 Can you tell me anything more about the project than what I see on the campaign site?

2 Why does crowdfunding interest you?

3 Has anyone shown interest in your project before you listed it on a crowd-funding site?

4 How long have you been working on this project?

5 Do you have friends and family members backing your plans for the project?

6 Do you have any funding besides what you are earning through the site?

7 Besides actually producing the project, what are your future goals?

8 How will you promote the project after the campaign is over?

9 What will you do if the campaign fails?

10 If the campaign is a success, what will be the most challenging part of your project?

Chapter 3

A Closer Look at Patreon

Patreon, like Kickstarter, aims to help creative people, or content creators, as they call them, fund projects. This also assists them in gaining attention and fans. The site is a mix of a typical crowdfunding platform with an old-school patronage slant. William Shakespeare and Leonardo da Vinci were just a few of the classic artists who had patrons. These patrons regularly funded all of the work they created, not just on a project basis.

As the Patreon site explains, "We think content creators are some of the most talented, interesting and deserving people on the planet. They spend hours, days, months, and dollars on projects that their fans and supporters have been waiting to see, just *because*. These creators start out sitting in front of their computers (probably in boxers) editing things that would only be seen by few." Patreon's niche, though, is that each project is seen as a minibusiness or a hobby that the creator wants to grow into a business. The team of people who work at Patreon want to help content creators turn these ideas into something real that can be as popular as possible.

Content creators use Patreon to get paid for creating the things they are already creating. These can include webcomics, videos, video games, songs, and much more. Fans may pledge a few bucks per month, or they may pay for each new product release. This way the creators get paid every month or every time they release something new.

Through Patreon, fans become real-life patrons of the arts. They don't just pay for a project. They pay to have the creators create more of their own content they enjoy. The pledge amounts tend to be low since fans pay on an ongoing basis. The average Patreon supporter donates about $7 for each creation. For example, a fan may pledge $7 for each video. If the creator releases four videos in a month, then the fan's credit card is charged a total of $28 for that month. This enables creators to get paid regularly if they

Cartoonist Zach Weinersmith of "Saturday Morning Breakfast Cereal" shows off his drawing of the wild Baguette Boar. He has thousands of patrons who provide funds each month so he can focus on creating new projects.

keep producing. Such a thing is rare for artists. Patreon allows artists to concentrate on their work. They do not have to get too distracted with how they'll find funding (or money to eat!) as they keep producing new content.

From the site's start in 2013 through April 2016, fans have given more than $50 million to creators. One of the site's regularly featured creators is Zach Weinersmith. He is a cartoonist and writer who produces the daily web comic "Saturday Morning Breakfast Cereal" (SMBC), among other things. By April 2016, he had 3,689 patrons. They pledged $8,840.06 each month to see his comics. "Patreon has been huge," he explains on the site. "[The funding] cascaded through my entire business. Making money from Internet content has gotten trickier over time, but Patreon has really reversed that trend. It's a very simple, very stable form of revenue."

Who Runs It

Patreon took shape in May 2013. It's led by developer Sam Yam and artist Jack Conte. Conte wanted to find a way to make a living from creating his popular YouTube videos. In August 2013, the company got a financial boost of $2.1 million. Venture capitalists and other wealthy people funded it, believing that it was a smart idea for a startup.

The following year, the site really took off. More than 125,000 fans had agreed to support content creators. This encouraged venture capitalist Danny Rimer to give it a $15 million shot in the arm. Such a boost helped the site expand even more. Other venture capitalists brought in another $30 million in 2016. With all this funding, Patreon can do plenty of things to expand and increase what it offers content creators to expand their businesses. Most of the funding through 2016 has gone to recruiting more staff for its engineering and product teams. Service offerings have also been expanded. In addition, they have paid more attention to making their website easier and better for creators and consumers. One of the most important ways to do this has been through mobile development of its app.

Musician/songwriter Jack Conte cofounded Patreon (www.patreon.com) to help creative people like himself fund YouTube (www.youtube.com) videos and other vehicles of expression.

Today, the site operates from an office in San Francisco, California. Like Kickstarter, it has a mostly young staff. Each member of the staff is featured proudly—each with personal photos and bios—on its site.

The site has not, however, always had smooth sailing. In October 2015, hackers broke into it. They took and published around fifteen gigabytes of private information. This included passwords, donation records, emails, and private messages.

How It Works

Creators set up a page on Patreon's website. There, fans can find them and donate funding per project or per month. Sometimes the content creators offer only one donation option, but donors are able to set maximum limits.

Fans can fund artists whose work they enjoy on Patreon (www.patreon.com). The site helps artists reach and build on their fan base in an organized way, so their work is regularly funded.

Patreon is different from Kickstarter. Content creators don't have to "start over" to find funding each time a new project is created. They can just keep creating. Hopefully this will help build them a fan base.

In most cases, fans pledge between $1 and $100 per month or per project. This results in many people pledging smaller amounts than fans on Kickstarter. Yet, like Kickstarter, Patreon encourages creators to provide rewards. They believe that rewards keep patrons happy and willing to continue their support. Also, Patreon take a 5-percent commission on pledges. Processing fees for credit cards, PayPal, and the like are taken from the creator's donations, too.

Creators like the personal connection the site gives them with fans, not just the financial support. "There is no-one controlling the relationship between my community and me," explains South African Nate Maingard on hypebot.com. He is a Patreon creator and singer-songwriter. "We talk about what interests us, share what we care about, and exchange value in a way which works for us. No labels or corporates to get in between us."

Patreon Success Stories

Many of Patreon's creators develop videos on YouTube. Others are visual artists, web comic artists, musicians, podcasters, and more.

Classic Game Room is a video game review podcast. It earns more than $10,000 per month on Patreon from about 1,300 patrons. Among the podcasts the creators have produced or promised: "Why *Sea Genesis* is the best video game system in the history of ever," "Records: the vinyl frontier," and "My love affair with *Star Wars*."

Kinda Funny is a four-person team that creates animated videos and podcasts. Their content exists thanks in part to more than seven thousand patrons who give about $34,000 per month. The four creators came up with their idea for Kinda Funny while working at the games and entertainment company website IGN.com. Thanks to Patreon, their decision to leave their jobs behind to work on Kinda Funny full-time seems to have made sense.

Singers Avi Kaplan, Kirstin Maldonado, Scott Hoying, Mitchell Grassi, and Kevin Olusola reach fans of their group Pentatonix on Patreon. Fan-funding has helped the group produce music videos and other projects.

Music group Pentatonix are set up on Patreon to produce a video or two each month for fans. The American a cappella group averages more than $19,000 from more than three thousand pledges for each video made.

File   Edit   View   Favorites   Tools   Help

HOW TO GIVE TO PATREON

How to Give to Patreon

The first thing you need to do is find creators whose work you like most. This can be done by reviewing featured creators on a list that is picked by Patreon staffers. You may also simply type keywords into the site's main search box. The site's blog, Twitter feed, and Facebook posts also feature new and exciting creators.

Besides finding creators making things you enjoy, you may choose them based on their rewards. Each creator develops a unique set of rewards. Creators do this in addition to the actual content you pay to have them create. These can include tutorials, behind-the-scenes information, or images. Bonus content (more than what is promised each month) and having your name in the credits are also offered often.

That boils down to about $5 from each patron. Plus, the group's talent and success has brought them worldwide attention and two Grammy awards.

Do-It-Yourself

Patreon's blog provides a lot of helpful information about how to develop and create project content. It also informs readers about how to build continued success. One of the first things creators must decide is if they will charge per project or per month. The site recommends that creators who plan to release more than four pieces of content per month should request monthly donations. In fact, 80 percent of fans donate per month. This may be so that they can control how much they contribute on a regular basis. Fans may be most comfortable knowing they will receive a specific minimum amount of content each month.

MYTHS & FACTS

MYTH When you contribute to a crowdfunding campaign for something being created, you own part of the completed project.

FACT All content creators hold onto their intellectual property rights. That means they hold the patents, trademarks, and copyrights. A crowdfunding site is not meant to take the place of a producer or a publisher. It is simply a link between people with ideas and backers with money.

MYTH People who contribute to campaigns risk nothing.

FACT Many websites will not release collected funds to campaigners unless a set amount is met. Still, there are risks to those who contribute. A project might get fully funded. But the sites can't guarantee that the people who create and promote campaigns will fulfill reward promises or that they will do so in a set amount of time.

MYTH You need a lot of money to start a crowdfunding campaign.

FACT This is not really true. Many sites require campaigners to pay to list their projects, though. That said, you do need ideas and something to show that will interest contributors. Many successful campaigns have proven that you also need a plan for rewarding contributors.

Chapter 4

The Future of Crowdfunding

Trying to see what's next for crowdfunding is like looking into the internet's future. Crowdfunding depends not only on word of mouth. It also relies more and more on social and news media. Social media has enabled everyday people to let others know about their needs. This allows individuals and small businesses to find new ways to reach interested people. At the same time, online news sources find an overflowing well of inspiring stories in crowdfunding campaigns. The people who run these campaigns and

The Pet on Wheels (POW) carrier for motorbikes and bicycles was produced and sold around the world thanks to Kickstarter funding.

their ideas help reporters fill the demands of the twenty-four hours a day, seven days a week news cycle.

Bringing in the Pros

One of the keys to successful crowdfunding is finding the right audience for each project. Many crowdfunding sites are now building platforms that enable campaigners to learn more about the site's audience. More importantly, they can also learn about the people who are interested in a campaigner's specific project. They can flag popular early pledgers who can lead campaigns to even more backers.

Marketing companies are also looking at ways to use crowdfunding. Many digital marketing companies now have crowdfunding teams. They are focused on helping clients use these sites as promotion. Then they help their clients target media coverage after the project is funded.

One such marketing company is Agency 2.0. This Los Angeles-based company shapes crowdfunding campaigns for clients. In its first five years in business, the company managed more than two hundred campaigns. "Our clients are great at creating new products, but have no experience with crowdfunding," says founder Chris Olenik. He was quoted by *Entrepreneur* magazine in 2016. "We have the processes in place to deliver a successful campaign."

Agency 2.0 and marketing agencies like it can handle a variety of crowdfunding tasks. These range from writing sales pitches and shooting videos to finding new backers. In return, most agencies charge setup fees. They may also require a percentage of the total campaign funds raised. This tends to amount to between 3 percent and 20 percent.

Never Too Big to Fund

Crowdfunding has been amazing for small, little-known players. Their audience and businesses often grow as a result. Yet bigger players are getting involved more and more.

Sony's Wena (Wear Electronics Naturally) smartwatch was launched on the international electronics giant's own crowdfunding site, First Flight (https://first-flight.sony.com).

"Corporations are realizing there is a lot of social engagement on crowdfunding platforms that can drive corporate innovation and offer alternatives to focus groups," says Richard Swart to *Entrepreneur*. Swart is a global finance researcher at the University of California, Berkeley's Haas School of Business.

To avoid backlash and help pledgers keep an open mind about new projects, some corporations use other names. These can be the names of their smaller member companies. One example of this occurred in 2015. Media and technology giant Sony ran a crowdfunding campaign for an

File   Edit   View   Favorites   Tools   Help

    HOW THE JOBS ACT HELPED CROWDFUNDING

How the JOBS Act Helped Crowdfunding

A government that aids entrepreneurs must pass laws to help their businesses grow, too. One such measure was the Jumpstart Our Business Startups (JOBS) Act. President Barack Obama signed it into law in 2012. Additional amendments kept it running through 2015.

The final pieces of the JOBS Act became law just six days before the megapopular Pebble Watch campaign launched on Kickstarter. JOBS was designed to make nontraditional loans easier. One example was crowdfunding. JOBS makes it easier for the people who run small businesses to find new outlets for funding. It also aids in setting up these businesses. Such efforts allow small businesses to stay private longer. They can also raise up to $1 million each year with fewer tax penalties and have as many as two thousand investors.

President Barack Obama shakes hands with politicians after signing the Jumpstart Our Business Startups (JOBS) Act in the White House Rose Garden on April 5, 2012.

e-ink concept watch. E-ink offers paperlike display technology. Sony ran this campaign on a Japanese site. It was not called a Sony campaign. Instead it was listed as being from a subdivision of the company, Fashion Entertainments, which develops wearable devices.

Growth and More Growth

A little over five years ago, crowdfunding had a small impact on business. It was seen as the realm of indie artists. Now it has entered mainstream culture by generating billions of dollars for many different purposes. Video game makers create games like *Star Citizen*. Universities fund research projects. One of these projects is a mission to the moon! Politics has gotten on the bandwagon, too. A SuperPAC is a large independent action group that helps politicians raise money. One of them, Mayday, has raised millions through crowdfunding.

Huge online companies are also joining in. Examples are Amazon, Ebay, Etsy, PayPal, and Stripe. They are working on bringing crowdfunding into their sites. How this will play out in the end is still unclear. The outcome is sure to come sometime soon, though.

Getting a Piece of the Pie

Reward-based crowdfunding sites are likely to continue to grow. Examples are the listed Kickstarter and Patreon. But equity-based crowdfunding is gaining ground. The passage of the JOBS Act in the United States has helped small-money investors. They can now easily buy stakes in startup companies. Not so long ago, investing in the stock of a startup was only for the wealthy. This puts decision-making power in the hands of a new group: middle-class people.

One early example of startup crowdfunding is iConsumer. "Equity crowdfunding gives us a chance to include all of our customers as owners," says Robert Grosshandler to the business magazine Inc. in 2016. He is the founder of iConsumer. "Even better, we're able to offer the 99 percent [those who are not the richest 1 percent of Americans] a chance to be part of the Wall Street world, without risking any cash."

As crowdfunding grows more popular, entrepreneurs and websites will become bolder. They will continue to explore how to use the model. It's clear now that no project can be too big, too small, too personal, or too quirky. Each of these can gain crowdfunding money and attention. Crowdfunding has few limits in a world where money and fame can turn dreams into reality.

GLOSSARY

all-or-nothing A funding requirement in which no one is charged for a project pledge unless it reaches its goal.

backers People who pledge money to campaigners.

campaigner This is the person or people who start the project and come up with the plan to fund it. Also known as the creator.

crowdfunding The practice of seeking financial contributions from a large number of people, especially through the internet.

donations Things such as money, food, clothes, and so on that you give in order to help a person or organization.

entrepreneur A person who starts a business in order to make money.

funding goal The amount of money that a creator needs for a project.

fundraising An activity done to collect money for a charity, organization, or project.

patron A person who gives money and support to an artist, organization, or other entity.

platform The computer network and equipment using a certain operating system. The staff and technology behind Kickstarter and Patreon are also considered a platform.

pledge A promise to give money.

podcast A program, typically with music or talk, made available in digital format for download over the internet.

project A plan with a clear goal that a campaigner would like to bring to life.

rewards Things or experiences promised to people who pledge money.

social media Forms of electronic communication such as websites for social networking and microblogging through which users create online communities.

startup A new business that is often technology oriented.

viral Quickly and widely spread, usually through the internet.

FOR MORE INFORMATION

Council of Economic Education
122 East 42nd Street, Suite 2600
New York, NY 10168
Phone: (212) 730-7007
Website: http://councilforeconed.org
The Council for Economic Education focuses on the economic and
    financial education of students from kindergarten through high
    school. The organization provides training to teachers and
    resources to encourage young people to learn about the economy
    and financial topics

International Child Art Foundation
PO Box 58133
Washington, DC 20037
Phone: (202) 530-1000
Website: https://www.icaf.org
The International Child Art Festival is an organization that seeks to
    nurture children's creativity and help them develop empathy through
    art. In the kids' section of the site, you can view *ChildArt* magazine
    as well as an online gallery of young people's art from around
    the world.

Money Management International
14141 Southwest Freeway, Suite 1000
Sugar Land, TX 77478-3494
Phone: (866) 889-9347
Website: http://www.moneymanagement.org
Money Management International seeks to improve lives through financial
    education. In the Financial Education section of the site, there is a

section called Youth and Money that offers articles on finance topics for young people.

National Crowdfunding Association of Canada
1240 Bay St., Suite 501
Toronto, ON M5R 2A7
Email: casano@NCFACanada.org
Website: http://ncfacanada.org
The National Crowdfunding Association of Canada provides loads of
information for those interested in finding funding as well as though
who hope to donate. The nonprofit aims to provide education,
leadership, and advocacy in the crowdfunding industry.

National Endowment for Financial Education
1331 17th Street, Suite 1200
Denver, CO 80202
Phone: (303) 741-6333
Website: http://www.nefe.org
The National Endowment for Financial Education provides a wealth of
financial information for high school and college students, as well as
adults. The site includes a link to Spendser.org, a teen-oriented site
with features that help them to be smart with their money.

Office of the Privacy Commissioner of Canada's Youth Privacy Initiative
30 Victoria Street
Gatineau, Quebec
K1A 1H3
Phone: (800) 282-1376
Website: https://www.priv.gc.ca/youth-jeunes/index_e.asp

The Canadian government provides information and tools about youth privacy on digital technology. Videos and rules for guidance are featured on the site.

Websites

Because of the changing nature of internet links, Rosen Publishing has developed an online list of websites related to the subject of this book. This site is updated regularly. Please use this link to access this list:

http://www.rosenlinks.com/DIL/Kick

FOR FURTHER READING

Cebulski, Aimee. *Kickstarter for Dummies.* Hoboken, NJ: Wiley/For Dummies, 2013.

Cindrich, Sharon. *Smart Girls' Guide to the Internet.* Middleton, WI: American Girl, 2012.

Engdahl. Sylvia. *Internet Activism.* Farmington Hills, MI: Gale Group, 2013.

Espejo, Roman. *Policing the Internet.* Farmington Hills, MI: Gale Group, 2012.

Gerber, Larry. *Cited! Identifying Credible Information Online.* New York, NY: Rosen Publishing, 2010.

Hand, Carol. *How the Internet Changed History.* Minneapolis, MN: ABDO Publishing, 2015.

Lennon, Patty. *The Crowdfunding Book: A How-to Book for Entrepreneurs, Writers & Inventors.* Washington, DC: Difference Press, 2014.

Meyer, Jared. *Making Friends: The Art of Social Networking in Life and Online.* New York, NY: Rosen Publishing, 2011.

Neiss, Sherwood. *Crowdfunding Investing for Dummies.* Hoboken, NJ: Wiley/For Dummies, 2013.

Reedman, Jeri. *Everything You Need to Know about Staying Safe in Cyberspace.* New York, NY: Rosen Publishing, 2011.

Steinberg, Don. *The Kickstarter Handbook: Real-Life Success Stories of Artists, Inventors, and Entrepreneurs.* Philadelphia, PA: Quirk Books, 2012.

Swanson, Jennifer, and Glen Mullaly. *How the Internet Works.* Mankato, MN: Child's World, 2012.

Wiener, Gary. *The Internet.* Farmington Hills, MI: Greenhaven Press, 2010.

Wolny, Philip. *Google and You: Maximizing Your Google Experience.* New York, NY: Rosen Publishing, 2011.

Young, Thomas Elliott. *The Everything Guide to Crowdfunding.* Avon, MA: Adams Media, 2013.

BIBLIOGRAPHY

BBC News. "The Statue of Living and America's Crowdfunding Pioneer."
April 25, 2013, http://www.bbc.com/news/magazine-21932675.

Collins, Katie. "Sexting, Vaping, Photobombing Reach Oxford English
Dictionary." *Wired* (UK), June 25, 2015, http://www.wired.co.uk/news/
archive/2015-06/25/sexting-vaping-photobombing-new-words
-oxford-english-dictionary.

Dredge, Stuart. "Kickstarter's Biggest Hits: Why Crowdfunding Now Sets the
Trends." *The Guardian*, April 17, 2014, http://www.theguardian.com/
technology/2014/apr/17/kickstarter-crowdfunding
-technology-film-games?CMP=EMCNEWEML661912.

Freeman, David M., and Matthew R. Nutting. "A Brief History of
Crowdfunding." November 5, 2015, http://www.freedman-chicago
.com/ec4i/History-of-Crowdfunding.pdf.

Fridman, Adam. "The Future of Crowdfunding." *Inc.*, January 25, 2016,
http://www.inc.com/adam-fridman/the-future-of-crowdfunding.html.

Gould, Jens Erik. "In Hollywood, Crowdfunding Isn't Just for No-Names."
TheFinancialist, September 12, 2013, https://www.thefinancialist.com
/in-hollywood-crowdfunding-isnt-just-for-no-names.

Graphtreon. "Top Patreon Funders." August 14, 2015 (https://graphtreon
.com/top-patreon-creators).

Hu, Cherie. "Crowdfunding Platform Patreon Raises $30 Million in Series B
Funding." Forbes, January 19, 2016, http://www.forbes.com/sites/
cheriehu/2016/01/19/crowdfunding-platform-patreon-raises
-30-million-in-series-b-funding/#13e4f83647ad.

Knowledge@Wharton. "Can You Spare a Quarter? Crowdfunding Sites Turn
Fans into Patrons of the Arts." Wharton University of Pennsylvania,
December 8, 2010, http://knowledge.wharton.upenn.edu/article/
can-you-spare-a-quarter-crowdfunding-sites-turn-fans-into-patrons
-of-the-arts.

Leather, Anthony. "The Record Kickstarter Project That Was Fully Funded in 34 Minutes: Meet LIV's GX1-A Swiss Watch." *Forbes*, February 19, 2016, http://www.forbes.com/sites/antonyleather/2016/02/19/liv -swiss-watches-gx1-a-kickstarter-project-fully-funded-in-34-minutes -was-a-record/#2086e32a7b42.

Maingard, Nate. "How Patreon Works For Me." Hypebot.com, January 22, 2016, http://www.hypebot.com/hypebot/2016/01/how-patreon -works-for-me-nate-maingard.html.

Prive, Tonya. "What Is Crowdfunding and How Does It Benefit the Economy." *Forbes*, November 27, 2012, http://www.forbes.com/sites/tanyaprive /2012/11/27/what-is-crowdfunding-and-how-does-it-benefit -the-economy/#62d467394ed4.

Prive, Tonya. "You've Just Crowdfunded Your Way to Success—Now What?" *Forbes*, December 5, 2012, http://www.forbes.com/sites/tanyaprive /2012/12/05/youve-just-crowdfunded-your-way-to-success-now -what/#6468b8b24cba.

Roberts, Daniel. "Tilt and the Future of Crowdfunding." *Fortune*, November 12, 2014, http://fortune.com/2014/11/12/tilt-future -crowdfunding.

Rodgers, Andrew. "Filmmaker Uses Web to Help Finance, Cast Movie." *Chicago Tribune*, June 11, 1999, http://articles.chicagotribune. com/1999-06-11/features/9906110076_1_kines-investing-film.

Warren, Christina. "A Guide to Kickstarter & Crowd Funding." Mashable, January 17, 2011, http://mashable.com/2011/01/17/kickstarter -crowd-funding-infographic/#b_6Gr2.i.Sqt.

Weisul, Kimberly. "In Crowdfunding, All-or-Nothing Campaigns Are More Successful." *Inc.*, June 19, 2014, http://www.inc.com/kimberly-weisul /why-your-crowdfunding-campaign-should-be-all-or-nothing .html?cid=em01011week25day19d.

Wertz, Boris. "The Future of Crowdfunding: 3 Important Trends to Watch." GeekWire, September 5, 2014, http://www.geekwire.com/2014/future-crowdfunding-3-important-trends-watch.

Wortham, Jenna. "Success of Crowdfunding Puts Pressure on Entrepreneurs." *New York Times*, September 12, 2012, http://www.nytimes.com/2012/09/18/technology/success-of-crowdfunding-puts-pressure-on-entrepreneurs.html?_r=0.

Zouhali-Worrall, Malika. "Comparison of Crowdfunding Sites." *Inc.*, November 2011, http://www.inc.com/magazine/201111/comparison-of-crowdfunding-websites.html.

INDEX

About the Author

Justine Ciovacco has written extensively for young people. Her writing has been published by Scholastic, Inc., National Geography, and Time for Kids, among others. She is a fan of crowdfunding and contributed to one of Spike Lee's films and other projects in the past, among other projects.

Photo Credits